I0031570

TEETHONOMICS

TEETHONOMICS

A PRIMER TO STARTING YOUR DENTAL BUSINESS

Dr. Hendrik B. Lai

MBA, MS-Management, Grad.Cert. -
Organizational Leadership, BDS, CM,
CPMgr, FCMI, FAIM, FInstAM, FIIDM,
AFCHSM

Mosen Fofel Publishing, Sheboygan, WI

COPYRIGHT

The information presented in this work solely and fully represents the views of the author as of the date of publication. Any omission, or potential misrepresentation of any persons or companies is entirely unintentional. As a result of changing information, condition or contexts, the author reserves the right to alter content at their sole discretion and impunity.

This work is for informational purposes only and while every attempt has been made to verify the accuracy of the information contained herein, the author assumes no responsibility for errors, inaccuracies and omissions. Each person has unique needs and this work cannot take these individual differences into account.

This work is copyright © 2017 by Hendrik Lai with all rights reserved.

Published by Mosen Fofel Publishing, Sheboygan WI, USA.

ISBN 978-0-6481100-1-9

ABOUT THE AUTHOR

Dr. Hendrik B. Lai is an entrepreneur, practicing dental surgeon, business consultant and an Adjunct Senior Lecturer at the College of Medicine and Dentistry at James Cook University. He is a founder and principal consultant at Schleining, Eldred, Lai and Company and serves as a Director of American Pacific Investments.

Hendrik is passionate about helping professionals build successful businesses and has been featured by dozens of media outlets including the Sydney Morning Herald, ABC, Channel Seven, Channel TEN, WIN, and the Australia Network. He has spoken extensively on health economics, strategy and health care access issues.

Hendrik and his wife, Sylvia, are the proud parents of Helena and Ethan and reside in Sheboygan County, Wisconsin.

DISCLAIMER

The publication is sold with the idea that the publisher is not required to render accounting, officially permitted, or otherwise, qualified services. If advice is necessary, legal or professional, a practiced individual in the profession should be ordered.

The information provided herein is stated to be truthful and consistent, in that any liability, in terms of inattention or otherwise, by any usage or abuse of any policies, processes, or directions contained within is the solitary and utter responsibility of the recipient reader. Under no circumstances will any legal responsibility or blame be held against the publisher for any reparation, damages, or monetary loss due to the information herein, either directly or indirectly. The presentation of the information is without contract or any type of guarantee assurance.

The trademarks that are used are without any consent, and the publication of the trademark is without permission or backing by the trademark owner. All trademarks and brands within this book are for clarifying purposes only and are owned by the respective owners, and are not affiliated with this work.

CONTENTS

INTRODUCTION

First of all, let me say: "Congratulations!" If you are reading this book, you are at least toying with the notion of starting your own dental business. The move from being a "technical" employee, by which I mean a dental practitioner, to being a business owner is a seismic shift and often requires a leap of faith. There will be numerous challenges that test your resolve and innovation, but the rewards that come with building a successful business are incredibly satisfying, both personally and professionally.

I have always had a bit of an entrepreneurial streak, with my entry into business coming at the tender age of seven. Rather than take the usual route of delivering newspapers or advertising brochures like many of my peers at that age, I approached the owner of a local entertainment group and offered my services creating their triplicate stock order books. My goals back then were very modest - to make enough money to buy my Mom a mother's day gift.

Being green to the world of business, and not having any understanding of the value of time, I priced my services a little low - earning the princely sum of one cent per book. Each order book took me twenty minutes to create. I did eventually make enough to buy my Mom an Elvis Presley cassette tape for mother's day.

Since then, I have started multiple diverse businesses, ranging from a sports nutrition business, to selling calendars door-to-door, to a piano tutoring business, and of course businesses in the dental space. Some of these start-up businesses gained more traction and success than others. However, I made sure I learned something from every one of my successes and failures,

INTRODUCTION

building my first seven-figure business from the ground up by the age of 26. I have been privileged enough to work with some great mentors and have created and run multiple seven and eight figure businesses since then. Over the years, I have grounded my experience with both formal and informal education and I am offering you the distillation of my business experience and education.

In my years as a practicing dental surgeon and business consultant, I have had the honor of teaching and mentoring a diverse range of clinicians as they have sought to transition into business ownership. For the most part, these clinicians have been masters of their respective crafts, excelling at the technical aspects of the profession and possessing outstanding patient care skills.

However, a common theme that I have come across is the general lack of business understanding. This is of course understandable when you consider the context that medical and dental schools are in the business of training

INTRODUCTION

medical practitioners and dental practitioners, not business people. With the advances in modern health care techniques and knowledge, there hardly seems enough time in a medical or dental curriculum to cover the technical and didactic nuances of the profession, let alone set aside sufficient time to provide even a basic business education. The down side of this is that when new physicians or dentists leave the cloistered halls of academia and begin their professional lives, they tend to wander aimlessly in the "real world", creating unnecessary stress and anxiety for themselves and their loved ones.

I have written this book to provide dental practitioners considering a transition to business ownership with a high level overview of the fundamentals of the business of dentistry, and an appreciation of vital considerations during the business startup phase. Although this book is written with a dental business context in mind, the principles it contains will be of great value to any technical worker transitioning to business ownership.

CHAPTER ONE:
Am I Ready to Start My Own Business?

This is one of the most common questions that I get asked by young (and some not so young) dentists who are eyeing business ownership. The short answer is that there is no right answer. I have spoken to many business owners and entrepreneurs and asked them when they knew they were ready to start their businesses.

One of the key messages that I have come across by talking to business owners, entrepreneurs, and have experienced myself, is that you will never be completely ready to start a business. That is to say, you're not likely to wake up one morning and decide: "Today's the day." More often than not, you will be toying with the idea of business ownership for some time, possibly even going so far as to discuss the idea with your family and close friends. Unfortunately for many would be entrepreneurs this is where the dream ends.

A great piece of advice, and certainly one which I agree with regarding when you are ready start a business is offered by Mor Assia, a founding partner at iAngels, an organization that specializes in connecting investors with startup companies. Mor says "you are ready to start a business once you've mastered a high degree of proficiency and expertise within your domain."

Now, for the dental practitioner this does not necessarily mean you need to have specialist level expertise in every aspect of dentistry. Indeed, if you attempted to develop this level of expertise in every domain of clinical dental practice, by the time you were ready to start your dental business you would probably be ready to retire from the profession!

Now, I can hear you asking: "When do I know that I've developed a high degree of proficiency?" The answer of course is: "It depends." Each individual will develop proficiency based on their access to the situations necessary to gain experience. However, for some general guidance, we can look to the work of psychologist Malcolm Gladwell who popularized the concept of the "10,000 Hour Rule".

The 10,000 Hour Rule contends that 10,000 hours of deliberate practice is necessary to develop expertise in a particular domain. You may not be familiar overly with the concept of "deliberate practice". Deliberate practice simply refers to practicing a given skill in a way that challenges your skill set as much as possible. In short, you need to be consistently pushing your personal envelope in order to gain proficiency.

CHAPTER ONE: Am I Ready to Start My Own Business?

Applying this to dental practice would mean that gaining experience in general dental practice, where you are exposed to a broad array of clinical procedures, is necessary to develop proficiency. So how long do you need to work to gain adequate experience and proficiency?

If we accept the general idea of the 10,000 Hour Rule, and use the following assumptions: an eight-hour workday and working 260 days a year (no vacations for you), you would need to work for around four years and 10 months to gain the necessary 10,000 hours of experience to develop proficiency in general dental practice.

However, natural ability, especially learning agility, does have a significant bearing on the development of proficiency. It would be safe to say that people who have managed to gain entry into, and graduate from medical or dental school have at least some affinity for learning. With this in mind, I would suggest that a minimum of around three years of clinical practice is necessary to develop proficiency in general dental practice.

CHAPTER ONE: Am I Ready to Start My Own Business?

Now, this is not to say that you cannot start your business before working for three years – there are no rules or laws precluding this. Indeed, perhaps more important than focusing on gaining technical proficiency is this piece of advice from Max Brown, founder of Silicon Beach Talent, a California based technology recruitment company. Max offers that the best time to start your business is when "the potential for rewards outweighs the risks." When exactly that time is will differ between individuals, and is something that only you can determine.

This translates to scanning the horizon for opportunities and making sure that you take advantage of those opportunities as they present themselves. By virtue of the fact that you are reading this book, I would say that you are likely to be emotionally and intellectually ready to start your own business. So the answer to the question posed at the beginning of this chapter is a qualified: "Yes, you are ready." Now you just need to start.

CHAPTER TWO:
Start With Purpose

We've established that you're ready to start a business, and I'm sure you're eager to begin. However, before we get into the nitty-gritty, it would be wise to explore what a business is. Once we have defined what a business is, we have an opportunity to understand why we are getting into business.

So, let's explore some of the more popular definitions of business that have shaped the practice and culture of business across the world. The Longman Dictionary of Contemporary English defines business as "the activity of making money by producing or buying and selling goods or providing services". The venerable Merriam-Webster English Dictionary offers the following definition of business "the activity of making, buying, or selling goods or providing services in exchange for money".

You will note that both of these definitions tend to place quite a degree of emphasis on the concept of money. There is of course nothing manifestly wrong with money – it is necessary in our modern lives and for the functioning of modern economies. However, what I have found is that businesses that exist solely to make money tend to make less of it, and also more often than not, don't know what to do with it when they do have it. Just look at the sustained success and growth of companies like Amazon and Apple for whom making money is a result rather than a goal, versus the more "traditional" companies like GE and Walmart that struggle to maintain growth and have seen significant drops in market capitalization.

CHAPTER TWO: Start With Purpose

Instead of viewing a business solely as an instrument to make money, I encourage you to approach starting your business with purpose. Why purpose? Purpose is important because it mobilizes people in a way that profit alone never will, and it is wise to remember that when we strip back all of the jargon and theory, all business is ultimately about people serving people in one way or another.

So what do I mean by purpose? Purpose is the reason your business exists. What problem does it solve for people? How does your business improve the world? Why do you do what you do? Why should customers use your business? In my experience, patients won't come to you because they want to make you rich.

As a dental practitioner, your business purpose statement will likely be very clear cut and easily defined. It may be something along the lines of "To optimize oral health so that our patients can smile more". You'll note that the purpose puts the emphasis on the customer, in this case your patient. Your purpose statement should express your business's impact on the lives of those you're trying to serve.

The purpose is different from the business's vision, mission and values, which we will explore in the next chapter. The vision, mission and values consider how the business should view itself whereas the purpose puts the emphasis on what the business does for someone else.

You might be asking: "Why does purpose matter? I just want to run a dental practice." Well, purpose matters for a number of reasons:

1) It causes your customers to feel a connection to your business and your products or services. When you can create an authentic connection to your patients, they will choose to buy your products or services even if they are not the cheapest offering.

2) It helps you recruit the right people. Although you cannot force your employees to share your

16

purpose, when you're building your business from the ground up, you have the opportunity to hire people with a common sense of purpose. When your employees are at odds with your purpose, your customers will know, and they will go elsewhere.

3) It allows you to develop a comprehensive and consistent narrative for your business. This helps your business to develop complementary services or products that fit the overall narrative of your purpose, giving you some direction rather than just moving on to the next shiny thing.

Remember, when setting your business's purpose ask yourself "why?" In today's highly competitive dental industry, the businesses that not only survive but thrive have one thing in common: the pursuit of an authentic purpose, running in tandem with the pursuit of profit.

CHAPTER THREE:
Vision, Mission and Values

Now we know why our business exists, let's start to look at the technical side of business. I mentioned in the previous chapter the concepts of the business vision, mission and values statements. If you have a look at almost any company's website you'll find some mention of these. So what are they and why do they matter?

The vision, mission and values statements of a business emphasize how the business views and conducts itself. Let's examine them in a bit more detail.

CHAPTER THREE: Vision, Mission and Values

The vision statement is an aspirational statement. It articulates what your business ultimately wants to be, or what you want your business to be in an ideal world. As a dental business, your vision might be: "To create beautiful smiles for every man, woman and child." Whatever it is, your vision needs to articulate what you want the future to look like for your business.

Vision statements should be revisited and reviewed regularly depending on what the purpose of the business is at the time and in the context of prevailing business conditions. Consider Stanford University's previous vision statement: "To become the Harvard of the West". Arguably, Stanford University has achieved its vision from that time becoming one of the top schools on the West coast. Individual schools in the university have since developed updated vision statements to suit their individual circumstances. In the same way, your vision must be responsive to changing business conditions. While the vision is forward-looking, it never hurts to look back to see how far you've come (you might be surprised) and review your vision based on what you've accomplished.

The mission of the business is something more immediate. The mission statement describes what the business does. Your vision will give rise to your mission in so much as what your business does (or does not do) should support the fulfillment of your vision. The mission is intended to provide focus to management and staff. It articulates what you do and whom you do it for. As a dental business, your mission statement might read something along the lines of "We're in the business of providing high quality cosmetic dentistry services to Dane County".

A business's values describe the desired culture. Values act as a behavioral compass for not only staff actions and interactions but for management decisions. Bright Horizons Family Solution, a provider of childcare and early education services, have their HEART Principles – Honesty, Excellence, Accountability, Respect, and Teamwork.

Values are important because they allow a business to intentionally shape the interactions between employees. The reality is that when staff members are looking for clues about how to behave they don't reach for a folder of written statements or the company intranet; they turn to other employees. By positively shaping these interactions, your business will have greater onboarding success with new staff members. In addition it has been shown that authentic business values contribute to greater customer satisfaction and staff retention.

Just as different individuals can share personal values, business values do not need to be specific to a particular industry. Very often, in a start up business, the business values will reflect the values of the founders. To give you some guidance, the core values at Schleining, Eldred, Lai and Company is:

- Courage: meet adversity head on.

- Wisdom: to turn adversity into opportunity.

- Integrity: to do the right thing – even when no one is looking.

- Fidelity: to make real our vision.

- Respect: to empower our stakeholders, both internal and external.

As you develop the values statement for your business, consider the values that you hold to be most important. These could be based on the values espoused by your profession or even your religious values – whatever you think will best guide the present and future behavior of your staff and the business.

The importance of developing an authentic set of vision, mission and values statements cannot be overstated. Vision is what you want your business to be in your idealized world. This in turn gives rise to your mission, which is what your business does currently or will do into the future. The mission should support your ability to realize your vision. Mission gives rise to your business's overall strategy. We will discuss strategy in the next chapter. Your business values provide the context for how your business will operate.

The decisions that you make about your vision, mission and values early on will set the tone for how your business and staff will act and interact with each other and your patients. Remember: "Any business is a series of actions which arise from a series of decisions". So, it pays to take a bit of extra time in the beginning to make the optimal decisions in the context of your goals and ambitions.

CHAPTER FOUR:
Charting Your Course

Now that we've set the vision, mission and values of our business, we're ready to delve deeper into the traditional science of business. In the previous chapter I mentioned that mission gives rise to strategy. Your business strategy charts the overall direction that your business will take in order to fulfill it stated mission. Ideally it will be based on a thorough strategic analysis of the overall industry.

CHAPTER FOUR: Charting Your Course

A common method of analysis used when considering business strategy is a Porterian analysis, sometimes called the Five Forces Model. This model was developed by Harvard economist Michael Porter and considers five essential forces that determine the "attractiveness" of an industry. Attractiveness can be read as "potential profitability" of the industry.

The five forces that are considered in this model are: the threat of new entrants, the power of suppliers, the power of buyers, the threat of substitutes and probably most importantly, the level of competition or rivalry in the industry. Let's take a closer look at the Porterian analysis of the dental industry. I have attempted to be as generic as possible, but specific countries and local markets will have different dynamics and interactions between the forces.

The degree of competition or rivalry can be assessed by considering a number of characteristics:

- *The number of businesses.* This may seem obvious, with the intensity of competition increasing as the number of competing dental practices increases. So, in an ideal world, having a monopoly or very few direct competitors is most favorable.

- *Market growth rate.* In a market with stagnant growth, the level of competition increases as the competing firms battle for market share. Conversely in a rapidly expanding market where there is plenty of revenue to be shared, the degree of rivalry is reduced - when the pie is getting bigger, everyone gets bigger slice.

- *Fixed costs.* High fixed costs increase the level of competition because your business needs to sell enough to achieve an economy of scale.

Producing more, and by extension increasing top line revenue, helps to offset the fixed costs. This is best illustrated by data from financial services firm Cain, Watters and Associates which shows that average fixed costs for a one dentist general practice is around 18.63%. Compare this to a three dentist general practice, where revenues increase threefold, but average fixed costs drop to 14%. The more that needs to be sold, the higher the level of competition.

- *High storage costs.* For the most part, dental products have high storage costs due to the perishable nature of dental materials. As a business, you will want to use your materials before they expire and you have to throw them out. Now if every other dentist is in the same position, and does the same thing, the level of competition increases.

- *Ease of switching.* Where it is easy for your patients to switch from one dental practice to another, competition increases. Broadly speaking, there are minimal switching costs in dentistry, so changing dentists is relatively easy for patients, even mid-treatment plan. This increases the level of competition.

- *Product differentiation.* Much as we might hate to admit it as dental professionals, a filling is a filling and a dental extraction is a dental extraction, at least in the eyes of the patient. It is exceedingly difficult to convince a patient that your amalgam filling is somehow superior to another dentist's amalgam filling. Basically patients don't know good dentistry from bad dentistry – unless of course they walk to the car park and the filling you've just put in falls out of their head. Low levels of product differentiation increase competition.

- *Exit barriers.* Dental equipment is generally regarded as having high asset specificity. This is because dental equipment is highly specialized meaning that it is difficult to repurpose for alternative uses and the market for resale is relatively small – it is likely the only people looking to buy dental equipment will be other dental practitioners. The high cost of abandoning the industry mean that a business may remain in an industry even when it is not profitable. These high barriers to exiting the industry increase competition.

Thinking about the dental industry and market in your specific location, and applying the above factors, you can characterize the level of rivalry as ranging from low to cut throat. A low level of rivalry or competition better positions your business in the industry. The ideal position is to have monopoly, where you are the only dental practice in the area.

The threat of substitutes is not a major issue in the dental industry. I'm sure we've all had the experience where a patient opts to see a physician to treat their toothache. In this case, the physician is a substitute. The treatment offered by the physician is usually a "Band-Aid" solution of antibiotics, and advice to go see their dentist. When a patient has a dental problem, they really don't have a lot of options except to see a dentist.

With that being said, in some jurisdictions "mid-tier dental providers", such as dental therapists and clinical prosthetists may offer a credible substitute to services offered by a dentist or dental surgeon. The presence of a close substitute affects price elasticity, effectively making it difficult to raise prices.

Buyer power can range from a *monopsony* where there is only one buyer but many suppliers, to near perfect competition with many buyers and many sellers. As a business owner, neither of these situations is ideal for you, as either extreme places significant power in the hands of your patients or clients to set prices.

Fortunately in the dental industry, there are many potential patients so except where a contract requirement exists, such as a preferred provider agreement or insurance arrangement, no individual buyer can greatly influence price. Additionally, there is no credible threat of "backward integration", as it is unlikely that your patients will open their own dental practice in competition with you.

The power of suppliers in dentistry stems from the situation that for many dental procedures, raw materials are needed - labor, dental materials, and sterilizing equipment amongst others. Where the supplier power is high, suppliers are in a position to capture some of your profits by selling these raw materials at a high price. Due to consolidation in the dental supply industry, we are seeing the power of suppliers increase resulting in lower competition between suppliers for your business.

Fortunately this increase in supplier power is effectively mitigated by the comparatively low cost of switching between dental supply companies and the generic nature of most dental materials and supplies. Further, there is minimal threat of forward integration, as it is unlikely that a dental supply company will purchase and operate dental practices in competition with you.

The final factor in our Porterian analysis is barriers to entry. Competition to your dental business comes not only in the form of existing dental practices, but also potential new dental practices. Fortunately, there are a number of characteristics inherent in the dental industry that tend to inhibit new dental practices from entering the market.

Perhaps the highest barrier to entry is government regulation. In many jurisdictions, government regulations prohibit dental practices from being owned by any person other than a licensed dental practitioner. There may also be zoning use restrictions that place a limit on the number of dental practices in a specific geographic market.

These regulations tend to work in favor of incumbent businesses. As someone looking to start their own dental business, these regulations may restrict opportunities for "green field" developments, meaning you may have to purchase an incumbent dental business.

Another barrier to entry, and one that may seem quite obvious is the requirement for "proprietary knowledge". In plain speak, in order to operate a dental practice, you can't just hire anybody off the street - you need to have a dentist with the requisite knowledge, training and licensure - this represents proprietary knowledge.

As we mentioned earlier dental equipment exhibits high asset specificity. Because this dental equipment is difficult to repurpose or sell, incumbent dental practices tend to quite fiercely resist new entrants from taking their market share, often through "entry-deterring pricing". How often have you seen incumbent dental offices offer special "promotions" when a new dental office opens nearby?

To bring it all together, we can assess the attractiveness of the dental industry by performing a Porterian analysis. Considering our five forces, we may come up with an analysis of the dental industry that looks something like this:

- Degree of competition is moderate to high, due to constrained market growth, a relatively high number of competitor dental practices, moderately high fixed costs, high storage costs, low levels of differentiation and high exit costs.

- The threat of substitutes of low. Generally speaking there is no credible substitute outside of the dental industry for dental care.

- Buyer power is low due to the presence of many patients in the market and the low threat of backward integration.

- Supplier power is low based on the generic nature of dental supplies, low switching costs and low threat of forward integration.

- The threat of new entrants is low due to the high barriers to entry in the forms of government regulation, required proprietary knowledge and high asset specificity.

From this analysis we can draw the conclusion that the dental industry is an attractive industry, where the overall industry is profitable. Indeed, this is likely one of the reasons you're considering starting your own dental business, and this analysis can help to validate your idea. Of course, you will need to perform your own analysis with information specific to your location and market.

CHAPTER FIVE:
Taking the First Step

Through our Porterian analysis we have established that the overall dental industry is profitable and it is worthwhile starting a business in this industry. So, what are your options for how you can get a cut of the dental industry's profits? This is where you decide upon your strategy to allow you to best position your business within the dental industry.

CHAPTER FIVE: Taking the First Step

Fundamentally, there are three generic strategies that a business can choose to pursue:

- The differentiation strategy

- The cost leadership strategy

- The focus strategy

Each of these strategies has its benefits and drawbacks and will be more or less appropriate depending on your specific strengths. Before we can decide on which strategy to implement, let's take a closer look at each of these strategies.

The differentiation strategy requires that you develop a service or product that offers something unique that is valued by your patients, or that your patients perceive to be better than your competition. As we've mentioned earlier, your basic dental service is essentially a commodity and is difficult to differentiate to your patients. However, it is possible to differentiate based on other aspects of your dental business, for example by leveraging technology to offer the convenience of same-day crown and bridge procedures.

A differentiation strategy allows you to charge a premium price for your service. When you're looking to offering something to your patients that you believe will add value and differentiate your business, I recommend that you ask these questions:

- "Will my patients notice?"

- "Will my patients care?"

- "Will my patients be willing to pay more for this?"

You should initially ask these questions internally and reflect on your answers. If your answers guide you to the conclusion that "Yes, I have something unique, that my patients will notice, care about and be willing to pay more for", you could further validate this by surveying potential patients.

The disadvantage of the differentiation strategy is that when you are the successful innovator, you will almost always be followed by imitators> This creates the situation where you will need to invest resources into continuously improving your product or service in order to maintain your competitive advantage.

Pursuing a cost leadership strategy means that you are seeking to be the industry's lowest cost producer for a given level of quality. In the dental field, quality means that you still need to meet regulatory requirements and adhere to accepted standards of practice.

Keeping costs as low as possible can be accomplished through improving process efficiencies, and gaining access to lower cost dental materials and labor. Due to the high fixed costs associated with dental practices, process efficiency optimization techniques tend to be very effective in dental businesses.

A cost leadership strategy gives you the flexibility to either set your fees at the industry average in order to earn a higher profit or to gain market share by setting your fees below the industry average. Be aware though that setting your fees too far below the industry average can back fire because potential patients often use price as an analogue for quality. So potential patients may assume that because you are charging a lower fee, your service must be low quality or that you are using low quality raw materials.

A focus strategy will see you target a narrow segment of the market and then attempt to achieve either differentiation or cost leadership within that specific segment. In this case, the idea is that by focusing on a small market segment and getting to know it very well, you can better serve the needs of that specific segment, versus being a mass-market business that tries to be everything to everyone.

Unfortunately, dental patients are for the most part not loyal, with 33% of dental patients in the US being happy to change dentists for a better deal. In the UK, this number is even higher, with 40% of adult dental patients ready to switch dentists. If you can effectively implement a focus strategy in your dental business, you'll be rewarded with exceedingly high levels of patient loyalty – this can deter other dental practices from attempting to compete directly with you in your chosen market segment.

The major disadvantage of the focus strategy is that because of the smaller number of customers that a segment represents, your volumes will tend to be lower than if you were a "mass market" dentist. This can make it challenging to achieve optimal cost minimization if seeking a cost leadership position within the market segment.

You're probably asking: "Which of these strategies is best?" As always in business, the answer tends to be: "It depends." None of the strategies are manifestly superior to any other. The choice of strategy will depend on your specific strengths and abilities as well as the characteristics of the dental market where you are. For example, if you can speak a second language fluently (a relatively uncommon strength), you may choose to focus on offering dental services to members of that community. On the other hand, if you are a highly experienced dentist who is able to plough through a high volume of patients, a cost leadership strategy may be more appropriate for you.

On a final note, I would caution you that generally the strategies are not compatible with each other, and to be successful over the long term, you need to choose one of these strategies at a time. However, there is no reason you cannot select a strategy initially and change direction if that strategy is not yielding your expected results. Indeed keeping an eye on the business horizon and making sure you have a responsive strategy is vital to business success.

CHAPTER SIX:
Setting Goals and Objectives

The business strategy you decided to pursue initially will provide you with guidance as to the specific goals and objectives you need to set. What is difference between a goal and an objective? You can think of a goal as the destination you want to reach at the end of your journey. For example, starting your dental business. Objectives can be likened to waypoints or progress markers along the way to reaching your goal. An example of this may be securing a lease on the premises or hiring staff.

Setting goals is very important not just for starting your dental business but also for success in everyday life. However many of us find it difficult to set goals, and as the saying goes: "If you don't know where you're going, any path will get you there." In order to optimize goal accomplishment, goals should be set to be challenging but achievable. In this chapter I will introduce you to a framework for goal setting, known as SMART goals.

SMART goals were introduced by George Doran in 1981. SMART is an acronym that has undergone numerous revisions over the years depending on the context in which it is used. However, perhaps one of the most widely accepted contemporary meanings of SMART is:

- Specific – in that a specific area is targeted.

- Measurable – a quantifiable measure of progress should be available.

- Achievable - the goal must be realistically achievable given known resources.

- Relevant - is the goal actually necessary to the bigger picture or the project as a whole? Striving to accomplish unnecessary goals is a waste of precious time and business resources. Charlie Munger, Warren Buffet's right hand man at Berkshire Hathaway, offers this piece of advice: "If something is not worth doing at all, it's not worth doing well."

- Time bound - the goal should be grounded in a time frame. Parkinson's law holds that: "work expands so as to fill the time available for its completion". Without a time frame there is no sense of urgency.

CHAPTER SIX: Setting Goals and Objectives

Now we know the elements that go into SMART goal setting, let's take a look at the example of extracting an infected wisdom tooth:

- The *specific* goal will be to remove the impacted lower left third molar in 30 minutes or less.

- We can *measure* time by looking at a clock. We will know the dental extraction has been accomplished when the tooth is removed in its entirety, and we may wish confirm this with an x-ray.

- Based on your training, skills, experience and the equipment available to you, is removing the tooth realistically *achievable* for you, or should you refer?

- Is removing the wisdom tooth important and *relevant*? Given that the tooth is infected, its removal would be considered to be a sound and reasonable treatment.

- We have set ourselves a *time frame* of 30 minutes in which to remove the tooth.

In this case, our goal of extracting the infected wisdom tooth in 30 minutes is a SMART goal. Now that our goal is set, we need to establish objectives. As we've mentioned, our objectives represent milestones to accomplishing our goal. Objectives may be based on process milestones. Let's again consider removing our impacted wisdom tooth. In this case, objectives might include:

1. Take an x-ray.

2. Gain patient consent (very important!)

3. Give local anaesthetic and achieve deep and profound anesthesia.

4. Raise a mucoperiosteal flap.
5. Remove bone and section the tooth.

6. Elevate the roots and smooth the bone.

7. Close the flap and secure with sutures.

By breaking down large and ambitious goals into smaller, more easily digestible objectives, we can create a series of milestones that allow us to measure how we are progressing as we strive towards our final goals. As you continue on your journey to establishing your business, some of the objectives that you will need to meet include:

• Locating a suitable location

• Deciding on what services to offer

- Securing finance

- Securing approvals from state/federal regulators and local government agencies

- Purchasing or leasing premises, plant and equipment

- Branding

- Fitting out and furnishing your dental practice

- Hiring staff

- Purchasing consumables

CHAPTER SIX: Setting Goals and Objectives

As you continue to learn more about starting your dental business, practice setting SMART goals in your everyday practice and daily life. You will find the exercise to be very useful in helping you to clearly define daily goals and objectives and will help you to cut away unnecessary, non-value adding or low value activities from your daily life. This will free up the precious time and resources needed to direct towards the 20 percent of activities that contribute to 80 percent of your business and personal success.

CHAPTER SEVEN:
X-marks the Spot – Selecting a Location

One of the most exciting and nerve wracking parts of starting your dental business (or buying an existing one) is selecting the location for your business. There are a number of factors, both personal and professional that you will want to consider when scoping out potential locations. In this chapter we will explore a data driven framework to selecting your business location.

Firstly, you will want to consider the demographics of the areas you are looking at for your business. A demographic analysis will consider the total population of the catchment area as well as other key demographic factors such as average household income, levels of dental insurance, median age and family make-up.

It is important that you consider the demographics in the context of the strategy you selected earlier. The demographics of your selected area should be compatible with your chosen strategy. For example, if you have decided to implement a strategy that focuses on providing expensive cosmetic dental services to your clients, you would most likely want to establish your business in a location with a high average household income. On the other hand, if you are looking to be a cost-leader, you might want to choose an area with a high uptake of dental insurance in order to enter into preferred provider organization agreements to optimize volume and achieve an economy of scale through insurance referrals.

An important complement to demographic information is psychographic information. Psychographics include information about the values, attitudes and aspirations of people in the area. This information is best obtained by interviewing potential clients. Why is psychographic information important if you already have demographic data?

Let's say you are considering starting a cosmetically oriented dental practice. Your demographic information may indicate the area that you are considering has a moderate median household income, so at first glance this area would not be an ideal fit for this kind of practice. However, your psychographic data might indicate that residents in the area are particularly concerned with health and appearance and spend a disproportionately large amount of their incomes of cosmetic products and services. This area now seems to be a more viable location in which to start your business.

In a nutshell, demographics give you the hard facts and explain "who" your potential buyer is; on the other hand psychographic data informs you about what moves potential customers to buy – it explains "why" they buy.

Another important factor to consider is the presence of competition. You will want to consider the number of other dentists in the areas you are looking at. The number of competitors should be considered in the context of the total population in the area – after all you will want to locate your business in an area with an adequate number of potential patients to sustain it and grow. It will be a very rare situation where you have an absolute monopoly, or where you are able to capture the entire market. But how many patients do you need?

While we don't have any solid data about minimum patient numbers specifically looking at dental practices – likely due to the wide variation in types of practices, we can look to general medical practice for some guidance. The 2014 American Academy of Family Physicians Survey found that there were approximately 2,367 people under each physician's care, and the physicians attended to approximately 19 patients per day. Notably at this level, some 75 percent of physicians described themselves as "overworked".

With this in mind, we can consider 2,300 patients to be the extreme upper threshold that a one-person full time dental practice can reasonably handle – although in my experience treating 19 patients a day on a consistent basis is more than likely going to result in rapid clinician burnout.

More reasonably if we use the assumptions of 12 patients per day, 260 working days a year, and an average of 2.6 patient visits per year we arrive at a more manageable 1,200 patients per year. In order to keep each full time dentist at or near full capacity, there should be a population of between 1,200-2,300 people per full time equivalent dentist in the area, assuming equal market share per dentist.

In a very broad sense, the best opportunities for location selection in terms of minimal competition and an underserviced market exist in regional and rural areas. Data from the University of Adelaide shows a significant maldistribution of dentists. Major cities have around 63.1 dentists per 100,000 people while in regional areas this falls to 38.2 dentists per 100,000 people, and in remote areas this falls again to 25.7 dentists per 100,000 people. A similar pattern of dentist maldistribution is repeated when we look at international data from the United States and Canada.

After utilizing demographic, psychographic and competitor data to decide upon the general area to establish or purchase your dental business, local factors become the dominant considerations. One of these considerations is co-location of your business within a larger health precinct or "mega-clinic".

There are a number of benefits of co-locating a dental practice near other complementary businesses, especially the potential for cross-referrals and increased "walk-in" appointments. Depending on your strategy, the presence of some businesses may negatively affect your ability to attract and maintain patients. Let's again consider our example of a business strategy focused on high-end cosmetic dentistry. Co-locating such a dental business with a cosmetic surgeon's office would be beneficial to both businesses through potential cross-referral traffic.

Visibility is a key local factor when considering the location for your new dental business. A location with high visibility to drive-by traffic and foot traffic is ideal. Visibility can be enhanced by good signage, however, these opportunities may be limited by local government restrictions and by-laws, and so it is worthwhile consulting with your local chamber of commerce or business development group.

When choosing a location for your fledgling business, price will often be a major consideration, but it should not supersede all other considerations. It is important to have a benchmark of the price per square foot (or square meter) for comparable businesses in your short-listed locations. This allows you to compare the value that a specific location offers. For example, a second floor premises may be significantly cheaper per square foot than a ground floor office, but visibility and accessibility are reduced and the opportunities for walk-in appointments from foot-traffic and drive-by traffic are less.

I have often found that businesses that try to save money by settling for less expensive locations find themselves in a situation of needing to spend any savings from the real estate (and then some) on additional marketing to try to compensate for poor visibility and client attrition to competing businesses with superior visibility and accessibility.

Although it may not seem relevant when you are just starting your business, I generally suggest that you consider the future growth potential for any short listed location. Ask yourself: "Will there be room for me to grow here?" At some point you will likely want to expand your dental business by adding additional operatories for associate dentists or perhaps you may want to add a dental laboratory. Due to the need for specific fixtures, plumbing and waste management requirements, it can be difficult for a dental practice to move premises.

This chapter has provided a crash course in selecting a location for your new business, or when purchasing an existing business. I have necessarily only considered business aspects for this analysis, but there may be personal factors such as proximity to family or schools that will influence the desirability of locations for your business and you will need to weigh these against the business and professional pros and cons that each potential location presents.

CHAPTER EIGHT:
Understanding Financial Statements

An understanding of finance is vital for any business owner, and is of particular importance during the start-up phase of your business. By no means do you need to have the finance or accounting knowledge of an accountant or an investment banker, but a fundamental knowledge of how to read and interpret the key financial statements is a must. There are three basic types of financial statements: the balance sheet, the profit and loss statement and the cash flow statement. We will explore these financial statements in this chapter.

The balance sheet, sometimes called the statement of financial position shows the financial condition of the business as of specific date, usually the end of a reporting period. This statement shows:

- Assets - this includes cash, inventory, plant and equipment.

- Liabilities - this is what the business owes, such as loans.

- Equity - this is what is left over after the business uses its assets to pay any liabilities. It represents what the business owes you as the owner.

Of course, there are more subtle sub-classifications of assets and liabilities such as current and fixed assets and current and long-term liabilities, but a full treatise on these is beyond the scope of this book. Suffice it to say that as a business owner, you want your business to have more assets than liabilities – translating into more equity for you.

The cash flow statement shows the movement of cash into and out of the business. This financial statement is very important for budgeting as it allows us to predict the movement of money into and out of the business. For all businesses, but especially start-up businesses, cash flow represents the life-blood of the business. The cash flow statement classifies cash flows into the following categories:

- Operating activities – this is cash flow from the business's primary activities. In the case of a dental business, this is the money earned and spent on the provision of dental services.

- Investing activities - this represents cash movements associated with purchasing or selling assets such as plant and equipment, but excludes inventory (which is usually reflected in operating cash flow).

- Financial activities - this includes incoming cash flow from raising capital through shares or debt, and outgoing cash flow from paying interest to debtors and dividends to owners.

The cash flow statement effectively gives you an idea of the amount of money in your bank balance. By comparing cash flow statements from different periods, you can predict when your business will see cash movements, allowing you to plan asset purchases and operational activities. For example if your cash flow statements show a consistent net outflow of cash during a particular period, perhaps due to interest payments, you may wish to consider holding off on purchasing new equipment during this period. You'll generally want to see a net cash flow into the business. Your business may then retain surplus cash, invest it or distribute it back to you the owner.

The profit and loss statement, sometimes called the income statement shows how the business has performed in terms of profit (or loss) over a specified period. This statement itemizes revenues and costs, and considers two basic elements:

- Income – this is all the revenue that your business has earned over the period and includes rental income, interest, and dividend income. In the early days of your dental business, you should expect that the majority of your income is going to come from the fees you earn by providing dental services to your patients.

- Expenses – are the costs incurred by your business over the reporting period. Expenses may include costs for labor, property rental costs, equipment lease, depreciation, laboratory fees and consumables.

To derive the net profitability (or lack thereof) of a business we subtract the expenses from the income over the given period. Analyzing the specific costs that your business is incurring provides the opportunity to "trim the fat" and run a lean operation. It goes without saying that as a business owner, you want to be in a position where your top line revenue (income) is greater than your expenses. Optimizing bottom line profitability enhances the equity that owners have in the business.

To pull it all together, for your business to be considered financially healthy it should ideally possess the following characteristics: a strong balance sheet where the owners have plenty of equity in the business, a net in-bound cash flow (although you may choose to have a neutral cash flow by distributing profits as dividends to owners rather than retaining the profits in the business), and a profit and loss statement which shows that income exceeds expenses and that the business is profitable. You should seek independent professional advice from a licensed accountant who can also help you prepare and further interpret these financial statements.

CHAPTER NINE:
Your Service Offering

Now that you have a fundamental knowledge of the key financial statements you will encounter, you should be able to create some financial projections for your business with the help of a licensed accountant. An important aspect to creating your financial projections will be to decide what you will be selling. You might think that the answer is pretty obvious, and *prima facie* in a dental practice it is - you will be offering dental services to paying patients.

CHAPTER NINE: Your Service Offering

In the early days of your dental business, particularly as you seek to maximize incoming cash flow from your dental fees, you will want to provide as broad a scope of dental services as possible. The scope of services you are able to provide will be dependent on your level of experience and training as well as any conditions of your licensure or registration.

All things being equal, by keeping as many services as possible within your practice rather than referring them out, you will maximize profit and will also reduce the risk of your patients leaving your dental practice. Unfortunately, dentistry suffers from one of the highest patient attrition rates in the health care industry, with a "normal" patient attrition rate of between 10-15% per year. Some estimates even put dental patient attrition rates as high as 20% per year.

One of the main reasons cited by dental patients for leaving a dental office is that the patients believed that the dental office did not offer the treatments they wanted. This may indeed be because the dentist simply did not offer the service and had to refer the patient externally, or more often it is because the dentist failed to communicate to the patient that the service was indeed offered. No matter the cause, the result is the same – a lost patient. Various estimates suggest that each patient that your dental business loses represents a lost lifetime customer value of between $10,000 and $45,000. Losing just ten patients a year could easily be worth nearly half a million dollars in lost revenue to your business, so it's definitely worth doing your best to minimize patient attrition especially early on.

With the above thought in mind, you're probably asking: "What services do patients want then?" The best way to find out the answer to this question is simply to ask existing and potential patients. I have conducted a number of surveys that have sought to understand why patients attend dental offices. The feedback from survey respondents falls into three broad groupings:

- To improve or maintain general health. Approximately 50% of survey participants responded that the primary reason they attend a dental office is for this reason. If you are looking to capture this market segment, it would be sensible to co-locate your dental business with complementary health businesses such as a family physician's office. A high proportion of these patients have dental insurance cover.

- To relieve pain or treat a toothache. This group represents an excellent opportunity to develop a loyal patient base. Nearly 28% of survey respondents identified this as the primary reason for attending a dental office. By relieving the patient's discomfort you have a prime opportunity to convert them into a regular customer. Many of these patients do not have dental insurance.

- To improve appearance. This group accounts for some 21% of respondents. Respondents in this group typically carry dental insurance, however do not tend to use it for appearance enhancing treatments, as most dental insurance plans do not cover "cosmetic" procedures.

I have repeated this survey a number of times over a number of years. The surveys canvassed several hundred patients across a number of dental practices in multiple states, each time producing fairly consistent results. The take away from this research is that in deciding upon your service offering it is wise to understand what your patients are looking for. For example, if you are not planning to offer cosmetic dental services, there is a potential that you will be missing out on nearly a third of the potential market.

Your stated strategy will also inform your business's service offerings to your patients. A strategy that focuses on providing high-end cosmetic dental services will necessarily mean that the services you offer will be skewed towards this – for example dental veneers, teeth straightening and dental whitening procedures. At the other extreme, where cost leadership is the driver and achieving high volume is necessary, the services you offer may be skewed towards dental extraction procedures, which are generally low cost and lend themselves to high volume production.

Your relationship with third parties will also greatly impact the services that you offer to patients. Preferred provider organization and dental insurance agreements may limit the type and number of dental procedures that you are able to offer. These agreements can require you to offer a certain number of dental services, most often "preventive services", to members or policy holders of dental insurance companies or plans at a specific pre-negotiated fee.

Even if you are not part of a preferred provider organization agreement, but simply accept dental insurance you might have restrictions placed on your service offerings by dental insurance companies. It is common knowledge that dental insurance companies employ complex algorithms to detect the provision of dental services outside of what they have decided to be a normal range. If you do happen to fall outside of their established "standard" range you may face sanctions or de-recognition by the insurer.

In deciding the types of dental services you will offer, you should take into consideration your individual training, experience and professional interests, and how these skills, and those of any staff you may employ, contributes to your business strategy. While it is ideal to provide as many dental services internally as possible, this needs to be weighed against risks associated with malpractice and associated litigation. I encourage you to only offer dental services for which you have been trained, have a demonstrated level of competency, and for which you are appropriately licensed and insured.

CHAPTER TEN:
Setting Your Fees

You've decided what dental services you will offer in your new dental business, and you will now need to decide how much you are going to charge for your services. For any business, setting appropriate prices for goods or services is one of the most challenging activities. You want to set your prices high enough that you can optimize your business's bottom line profitability, but you don't want to set your fees so high that you price yourself out of the market and lose market share.

CHAPTER TEN: Setting Your Fees

There are a number of methods used to set professional fees in the dental business context. Perhaps the most straightforward of these is to set your professional fees according to the customary fees of dental practices in your area. Many local dental associations publish an annual survey of dental fees that provides an aggregate summary of median fees for specific services as well as the professional fees for the top and bottom quintile of dental practices in the area. With this business intelligence you can set comparable fees to other practices or can choose to set fees at a discount to the market median in order to gain market share.

In a dental business, contemporary wisdom holds that you are fundamentally trading your time for your patients' money. If we accept this wisdom to be broadly true, another common fee setting method is to decide upon an expected hourly billing rate and set fees for individual dental services based on the time needed to perform those procedures. For example, let's say I am targeting billings of $400 per hour. It takes me approximately 30 minutes to do a one surface composite resin filling. If I were to set my fees according to time, I would charge my patient $200 for the one surface composite resin filling procedure. i.e. $400 x 0.5.

Although the time based billing method is simple to use, it tends to penalize proficiency. Consider if I am now able to do the same filling as before in 15 minutes and to the same level of quality. Under the time based fee-setting method I would now charge the patient only $100. Unfortunately, whether I can do the filling in 30 minutes or 15 minutes my consumables cost has not changed, so my profitability per procedure has now decreased.

On the other hand, if I take an hour to do the same filling, again to the same quality, patients would now be charged $400, certainly good for my per procedure profitability, but not exactly great value for my patient and perhaps enough them to look elsewhere for more affordable dental care.

A more sophisticated method of setting your professional fees, and one which I like to use, is the "cost plus" method. This method requires you to consider the total cost of providing a specific service. These costs can include labor costs, consumables, and dental laboratory fees. Once the costs have been established a profit margin multiplier can be applied to ensure that the costs are covered and the procedure is profitable.

Let's take a look at an example of a single surface composite resin dental filling. For the purpose of this example, we'll use these assumptions:

- The filling procedure takes 30 minutes

- Fixed overheads come to $100 per hour

- There is one dental nurse who is paid $20 per hour.

The table below shows an itemized consumables cost list for our procedure.

CONSUMABLE PRODUCT	COST PER PROCEDURE ($)
Local anesthetic	0.90
Topical anesthetic	0.31
Bracket table cover	0.59
2x2 gauze	0.03
Cotton swab	0.01
Rubber dam	2.27
Adhesive bond	2.71
Flowable composite resin	5.31
Composite resin	3.78
Polishing point	2.99
Sterilization pouches	1.05
Bib	0.59
Disposable plastic cup	0.05
Tray cover	0.37
Cotton rolls	0.06
Gloves	0.88
Micro-brush	0.14
Total	22.04

In this example, our consumables cost is $22.04, and based on our assumptions, the labor cost for the dental nurse is $10 and the fixed overhead cost is $50. Hence the total cost for this procedure is $88.04 ($22.04 + $10 + $60). We now need to apply an algorithm to this cost to arrive at our fee for the procedure.

A commonly accepted algorithm is to apply the "Rule of Threes". That is we multiply the cost of the procedure by a factor of three to arrive at our professional fee. In our example this would be $88.04 x 3. Hence, we arrive at a fee of $264.12 for our procedure.

Of course, the example above is for illustrative purposes only, and you will need to undertake a similar process for each procedure you perform using costs and a multiplier factor relevant to your situation. However, I have found that this three times multiple of costs generally results in fair professional fees for patients, without creating the perception of low quality, while still providing for solid profit for the dental business. Your strategy should also guide you - if you have a unique value proposition (you're differentiated) you may be able to use a higher multiplier. If your general thrust is volume (cost leadership) and want to attract more patients you may want to use a lower multiplier.

While it may seem tempting to try to undercut the competition to gain market share, this can have a disastrous impact on profitability, as you can expect any change in fees to be met with a change in profitability. Following is some modelling based on research performed by Eastman Kodak designed to determine the effects of various price decreases on profitability. The following data is based on the assumption of an initial 25% profit margin.

- A 5% fee decrease requires a 25% increase in sales to maintain the same level of profitability.

- A 10% fee decrease requires a 67% increase in sales to maintain the same level of profitability.

- A 20% fee decrease requires a massive 400% increase in sales to maintain the same level of profitability.

As you can see, decreasing your prices to gain market share means you will have to accept decreased profitability per procedure, with the hope that the gain in market share will provide sufficient additional volume to offset this reduced profit. However, remember that you are effectively trading time for money, so even if the increase in market share was realized, it would be very challenging to find enough additional time in the day to service this increased volume without employing additional staff which in turn adds more costs. The additional staff related costs your business incurs might be enough dilute any profitability gains.

Of course you should revisit your fees on a regular basis and adjust them depending on your business strategy and costs at the time – this will generally be an increase in price. Many dental practices opt to increase their professional fees yearly. I have found that increasing professional fees by a small percentage every ten months does not negatively impact price elasticity any more than does an annual increase, but it does provide a "bonus" fee increase over a five-year time frame.

CHAPTER ELEVEN:
Serving your Patients

The primary business of a dental practice is providing dental services to patients. On the surface, it may certainly appear to be that simple. However, when providing consulting and business coaching services to dentists and other health care professionals, one of the common things I hear is: "I'm offering all these great services, I have the latest technology, and my fees are low but I'm still not getting any traction with patients."

CHAPTER ELEVEN: Serving Your Patients

This chapter is not intended to tell you what clinical services you should offer in your dental business. That decision will largely be a function of your business strategy, your specific clinical skills and interests, and has been explored earlier in this book. Instead, I am offering a generic overview into what it is that health care customers, including dental patients want.

For the most part, dental and oral health professionals looking to start a business (or who have been in business for some time) are generally experienced and technically proficient at their craft. With this in mind, commonsense would dictate that acquiring new patients and retaining existing ones should be a no brainer. Unfortunately, as you are probably finding, most things in business are not so cut and dried.

Conventional wisdom would suggest that if a dentist's fees are competitive (perhaps even on the lower side of the market median), their technical skills are solid, they have all the latest and greatest technology, and their location is good they should have no problems in attracting and retaining patients - but what is happening when patients are not flocking through the doors, and the business is perhaps even losing patients?

Marketing and advertising can help with attracting new patients, but these activities don't really help with retaining existing patients. It is also relatively expensive to acquire new patients especially through traditional channels with it being generally accepted that you need to spend $4.00 to acquire a new patient, for every $1.00 spent to retain an existing one. So what is it then that prospective patients and existing patients consider to be important in a health professional's practice?

The answer to this question might surprise you. Let's take a look at the value elements that patients deem to be important when selecting and staying with a particular dentist. Much of this research is underpinned by the concept of the "Value Pyramid", developed by international consulting firm Bain and Company, which in turn draws inspiration from Maslow's venerable Hierarchy of Needs. In order of importance, these value elements are:

1. Communication. This may seem like a no brainer to patients, but it is a factor that tends to be overlooked by busy dentists. You should remember that when patients attend your dental practice, they will often be very vulnerable and they will be seeking reassurance from you as much as they are seeking treatment for their condition. In fact communication was rated as important by some 90% of survey respondents.

   From research I have conducted, I have found a very strong correlation between a patient's perceptions of the clinician's communication, how they rated their visit and their referral patterns to the dental office. From a patient value perspective this factor informs and reduces anxiety.

2. Pain control. Let's face it, many medical and dental procedures can be uncomfortable for patients and for the most part, no one likes to be in pain. It is no wonder then, that 73% of patients rated pain control as important

to them. Patients see value in this element as it addresses needs around reducing anxiety and reducing patient risk.

3. Safety and Infection Control. Beyond your business's basic duty of care to your clients, one of the key tenets of health care is *non-malfeasance* - or to do no harm. Most dental professionals would consider infection control to be a core competency for a dental practice, and patients see it no differently. Addressing this concern adds value by reducing risk, reducing anxiety and enhancing wellness. Nearly 73% of patients rated safety and infection control as important.

4. Technical Competence. This is probably the one factor that dentists and other health professionals tend to pay an inordinate amount of attention to, most probably because it is how *we* judge quality. The reality though is that patients expect only a minimum level of *perceived* technical quality and competence. Once that perceived

minimum level is met, any further gains in patient satisfaction are marginal, as patients find it difficult to accurately evaluate technical quality.

This factor addresses value derived from therapeutic value, anxiety reduction and quality. It may also add value by enhancing attractiveness depending on the specific services offered by your dental practice.

5. Convenience and Extended Hours. Research has found that three of the four least important factors when patients make a decision about their dentists were opening hours, waiting time and time spent with the dentist.

My research found that there was a weak correlation between clinical access and convenience and overall patient satisfaction. However, that is not to say that this factor should be ignored as it adds value by providing access, simplifying patient activity and reducing the effort patients need to expend.

6. Facilities. Again, this is a factor that dentists tend to give over an inordinate amount of time and resources to addressing. The reality is that the dental business's facilities are more important to the dentist and staff than they are to patients. Certainly, research suggests that facilities are not considered to be as important as other factors in determining patient satisfaction.

   Practice neatness, the comfort of seating, waiting room magazine selection, and background music have been shown to influence patients, but only to a minor degree. Survey responses suggest a weak correlation between facilities and overall patient satisfaction and referral patterns. Facilities contribute to value by addressing patient sensory appeal.

7. Cost/Price. For most businesses price cannot be ignored, but it comes in low on the list of factors that patients consider. For the most part patients use cost as a proxy for quality. The danger with setting your fees too low is that patients may assume that the quality of your care is inferior.

The two lowest-rated items for patients when choosing a dental practice are "Knowing in advance what the fee will be" and "Believing that the fees are appropriate". Given that cost is seen as a proxy for quality, patient value can be gained through thoughtful pricing strategies.

The seven factors mentioned above address certain consumer value elements. As a general rule, the more value elements that your dental business (or any business for that matter) can satisfy the greater will be your patients' loyalty and the higher your business's sustained revenue growth.

The take away message from all of this is that in order to serve your patients in a way that satisfies them, you do not necessarily need to spend a lot of money on having the latest technology, nor do you need to have the most fancy clinic facilities - you don't even need to be a phenomenal dentist.

CHAPTER ELEVEN: Serving Your Patients

Simply, you have to be willing and able to communicate with your patients in a way that treats them with dignity and respects their right to autonomy in choosing their treatment. We can conclude: "Patients don't know good dentistry from bad dentistry. All they know is whether or not you were nice to them and if you hurt them."

In my classes, I like to remind students that no matter the nature of your business, "People do business with people they like and trust". Hence the key to success in business is to be liked and trusted by as many people as possible. Keeping in mind the value elements you learned about in this chapter as you serve your patients will provide you with sound guidance in positioning yourself as the trusted dental authority to existing and potential patients.

CHAPTER TWELVE:
Getting Help

By now you have the probably come to the conclusion that there is a lot of work that needs to go into starting a dental business. It is very difficult to manage every aspect of the business, and often you will not have the expertise to perform all of the activities on your own. This is when it becomes necessary to bring on board team members to assist and support you.

CHAPTER TWELVE: Getting Help

In order to provide a clinical dental service you will generally need to at least employ a dental nurse. In the very beginning it is likely you will have some excess capacity in your appointment book so the dental nurse can also undertake reception duties. To control labor costs it is advisable to start dental nurses on a "casual" employment basis. Under these employment agreements staff are not guaranteed specific hours or days, giving you the flexibility to call on staff as needed, and only pay them for the time they work. Generally, staff employed on a casual basis are not eligible for vacations or sick leave.

The downside to this is that many jurisdictions require that casual staff be paid at a higher hourly rate to account for the loss of vacation or sick pay and to compensate for the absence of tenure. Further, just as you are under no obligation to guaranty a specific number of hours to casual staff, these staff are under no obligation to accept the shifts that you offer them. This can result in short staffing which reduces operational efficiencies and can detract from the patient experience - something that a start-up dental business can ill afford.

CHAPTER TWELVE: Getting Help

Broadly speaking though, most dental practitioners with at least a couple of years experience under their belts will have a firm grasp of the clinical aspects of dentistry (the line function) including the type of staff support necessary for specific procedures. However, an understanding of the staff functions, or back office support can be a little more elusive for a dental professional.

The line functions in a business are those business functions and the associated staff that are involved in generating income revenue for the business – that is they directly advance the business. Examples are sales people in a car dealership or the dentist and dental hygienist in a dental practice. Staff functions are not directly involved in generating revenue income but rather are those functions and the associated staff that support the activities of the line functions so that they can perform the activities that advance the business. Examples of staff functions include the finance, marketing and human resources departments.

CHAPTER TWELVE: Getting Help

In my experience, as a business owner you have one of two options when it comes to managing the business of dentistry. Firstly you can choose to be a completely hands on manager, being involved in every aspect of the business including the day to day operations of providing clinical dentistry and earning business revenue, to doing payroll functions, staff performance management and marketing. However, it is important to be aware that in choosing to undertake everything, you will be spending time performing non-revenue generating staff functions, taking time away from income producing activities like performing dentistry on paying patients.

In the early days of your business, where exercising cost discipline to save money is of paramount importance this makes sense. However, as the business grows you will need to weigh the opportunity cost of saving money on labor by performing staff functions yourself against the potential lost income. When the cost savings realized by undertaking staff function activities yourself is outweighed by the foregone revenue, it is time to hire outside help. Of course, you may wish to bring on board outside help to perform support functions from the very outset.

This brings me to the second option. In this case although you are the business owner in so much as you have equity in the business, you cede operational management decisions to someone else – usually a practice manager. The advantage of this option is that it frees up your time to generate income revenue and also provides a firebreak of sorts between you and the day-to-day business operations. The major disadvantage is of course the cost involved in employing someone as a practice manager.

So what should you look for when employing someone to work in your business? You are probably used to seeing recruitment processes that include a resume screening followed by an interview. Unfortunately, this method of recruitment yields highly variable results when it comes to job success. Using an interview for staff selection is likely to select a candidate who will be successful in the role in only three in ten cases. Selecting a candidate for a role based on experience is even worse, with experience-based selection yielding a successful candidate in only one in ten cases.

To assist my clients in selecting the optimal candidate for the roles in their businesses, I have developed a model underpinned by the works of Hunter et al, Chao et al, Asher and Sciarrino, and Cohen et al.

The best available research concludes that tests of General Mental Ability (GMA) should be considered the primary measure for hiring decisions, and that other measures can be used to supplement the GMA tests. The research found that using GMA tests and a secondary variable increases the validity of the secondary variable by up to 27%. The exception to this is age where no change in validity was found when combined with GMA. In fact age was found to have a negative correlation to job success.

With these research findings in mind, I recommend that when recruiting tea, members for your business, you include a test of general mental ability for all shortlisted candidates. How much difference does performing well in a GMA test make? From a monetary perspective, it has been found that for every standard deviation above the average that someone scores in a test of GMA, their performance output is 40% higher than a candidate with an average score.

Tests of GMA typically measure the following dimensions:

- General knowledge

- Social Intelligence

- Arithmetic

- Verbal

- Vocabulary

- Coding

- Detail orientation

- Spatial rotation

- Spatial reasoning

As a dentist, it is highly likely that you have taken a number of GMA tests, with examples including the Wonderlic Personnel Test, the Watson Glaser Test, Intelligent Quotient Tests, Graduate Record Examination and tertiary admissions tests such as the DAT, STAT, MCAT and GMAT

For a candidate performing to your selected standard on a GMA test, the choice of the secondary variables to be assessed during the recruitment process is job dependent. I categorize roles in dental businesses into three broad groupings along with recommendations for the secondary selection measures for each.

ROLE	RECOMMENDED SECONDARY MEASURE
Clinician	Work Sample, Integrity Test, Structured Interview
Administration	Integrity Test, Job Knowledge Test, Structured Interview
Auxiliary	Supervisor Rating, Integrity Test, Job Knowledge Test

This model does not consider cultural fit, and you should consider how well candidates for roles in your business will fit with your organizational values and how well they will work with other staff members (including you). If you have a strong authentic purpose statement, candidates that are a good cultural fit with a shared purpose will be attracted to your business.

The cost of employing the best candidate based on their performance in tests of GMA, secondary variable assessments and cultural fit can seem daunting. However it is wise for you to remember this: "If you think it is expensive to hire the right person, just wait until you see how much it costs when you hire the wrong person." As with clinical staff some of the costs associated with employing support staff can be minimized in the early days by employing people on a casual basis. Additionally outsourcing is often an option with staff functions, with it being quite common for start-up businesses to outsource activities such as marketing and recruitment.

CHAPTER TWELVE: Getting Help

While it is definitely good to be armed with the knowledge of best practice processes for hiring someone for your team, a question that is even more fundamental to getting help, and one that I am consistently asked by my clients is: "When should I look to hiring someone to help me in my business?" The answer I always give is a qualified: "As soon as you can."

My reasoning for this is that at its very core, a business can either give or take away three things from its owner: money, time and freedom. Your ultimate goal as a business owner should be to develop your business to a point that it is able to give you all three.

It goes without saying that you want your business to provide you with a source of income, be that through trading your time for money by performing dentistry or passively through distributions of business profit. By employing an associate or assistant dentist or perhaps a dental hygienist, you have the opportunity to increase your business revenue without a directly proportional increase in overheads. You may remember from an earlier chapter that the best way to reduce the percentage of fixed costs in your business is to increase revenue.

Conventional wisdom holds that in a dental business, revenue of around $1 million is necessary to achieve an internal economy of scale and the associated operational efficiencies, although this figure may be slightly different depending on your location. Your goal should be to ramp up your revenue to this level as quickly as possible. You can accomplish this through your dental fees or by increasing the volume of dentistry performed - or some permutation of the two.

I recommend that you match your supply capacity (that is your number of available appointments or trading hours) with market demand (that is the number of patients you see). As a guide, I have found that when you are at full capacity, meaning you're making prospective patients wait two weeks (not withstanding clinical requirements such as laboratory turn around times), for at least three weeks, its time to hire some clinical assistance for your business to help you crystallize this good will. Keeping patients waiting too long can see them seek dental care elsewhere.

Hiring someone to help you in your business gives you time. This might initially be at the expense of some money, but it provides you with the opportunity to spend time doing the things you enjoy, and allows you to work *on* your business rather than in your business. That is, by employing a clinical associate, you don't *have* to trade your time for money. You may even be able to take time away for a much-needed vacation or to undertake a course without having to worry about how your business is going to run while you are away.

Freedom is the ultimate resource your business can give or take. It is a function of time and money. Developing your business to a point where it provides you with both time and money gives you freedom. This could be the freedom to continue to "keep your hands wet" and do some clinical dentistry, not because you have to, but because you *want* to. It could be the freedom to spend time away from the business to give back to the community by teaching at a local university or volunteering to provide *pro bono* dental care to vulnerable community members. It could be the freedom to spend time writing a book on starting a dental business.

When you have taken the plunge and employed staff, you will need to develop an organizational chart showing the relationship between the various roles and staff members in your business. The organizational chart is intended to show reporting lines and helps to clarify the chain of command. While it may be tempting to have everyone in your business reporting to you, I would warn you that trying to directly manage too many people is time consuming and largely ineffective.

While there are some quite complex algorithms available for determining how many people should report to involving calculating potential cross relationships between individuals and direct group relationship, these are probably excessive and unnecessary for a typically sized dental business. Generally, I have found that an optimal number of direct reports is between three and eight people - this is your "span of control".

A span of control with less than three people is typically cost prohibitive and can lead to micromanagement of tasks - this can lead to you delegate less, largely obliterating the advantages of the time efficiencies gained by hiring staff. Having more than eight people directly reporting to you can lead to you being overloaded and your employees feeling they don't have enough support resulting in reduced morale and job satisfaction.

When developing your organizational chart, you should try to avoid a situation where staff members report to multiple people as this can lead to poor communication and confusion. The worst-case scenario of the "matrix structure" is where the one direct supervisor disagrees with another direct supervisor resulting in gridlock in decision-making and an unhealthy competition between the supervisors. I have provided an example of simple organizational chart for you to use as a template in your business below:

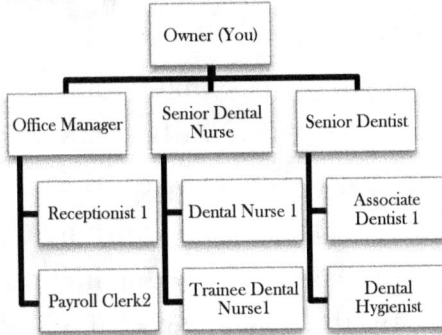

```
                        ┌─────────────┐
                        │ Owner (You) │
                        └──────┬──────┘
         ┌─────────────────────┼─────────────────────┐
┌────────┴───────┐   ┌─────────┴──────┐   ┌──────────┴─────┐
│ Office Manager │   │ Senior Dental  │   │ Senior Dentist │
│                │   │     Nurse      │   │                │
└───────┬────────┘   └────────┬───────┘   └────────┬───────┘
        │                     │                    │
┌───────┴────────┐   ┌────────┴───────┐   ┌────────┴───────┐
│ Receptionist 1 │   │ Dental Nurse 1 │   │   Associate    │
│                │   │                │   │   Dentist 1    │
└───────┬────────┘   └────────┬───────┘   └────────────────┘
        │                     │
┌───────┴────────┐   ┌────────┴───────┐   ┌────────────────┐
│ Payroll Clerk2 │   │ Trainee Dental │   │    Dental      │
│                │   │    Nurse1      │   │   Hygienist    │
└────────────────┘   └────────────────┘   └────────────────┘
```

Early on in your business, it can help to reach out to a business coach or consultant. Typically your business coach or consultant will be an experienced entrepreneur or businessperson in his or her own right. This coach can help you to brainstorm ideas and act as a sounding board to bounce ideas off. Perhaps most importantly though, a business coach will hold you and your team accountable for accomplishing objectives and goals. It's easy to break promises to ourselves, but when we involve someone else we tend to keep them - think about all the early morning workouts you promised yourself you'd do!

On a related note, many lending institutions will want to see a strong management team in your business before they will extend you finance. The reason for this is that banks and similar institutions are generally more comfortable lending money to businesses that are lead by a management team with experience and a track record of success as these businesses are seen as less risky. In the early days of your business, it may be necessary for you to acquire some immediate managerial experience by contracting an experienced *locum tenens* manager to allay lending institution concerns.

CHAPTER THIRTEEN:
Benchmarking

You may have heard the quote: "What gets measured gets managed". This quote is attributed to management expert Peter Drucker and it is definitely a truism in business and dental businesses are no different. Regularly measuring your key performance indicators will give you an idea of how your business is performing and allow you to make adjustments to your operations in a timely manner. Although it is good and well to measure your performance, you need something to compare your performance against. This is where benchmarking comes in.

So what exactly is benchmarking? The American Society for Quality defines benchmarking as the "process of measuring products, services, and processes against those of organizations known to be leaders in one or more aspects of their operations". This represents a rather austere definition of benchmarking, but is definitely a useful point to start from. Using this definition you want to compare your business performance to industry leaders or more commonly, accepted industry norms.

Benchmarking can be categorized according to the level it occurs at. Internal benchmarking is undertaken within your business, usually between business units or in a dental context between practices within the same group. Competitive benchmarking occurs between you and your competitors. As a start-up dental business, it is likely that you will not need to undertake internal benchmarking, so I will focus on competitive benchmarking of metrics against accepted industry norms. For your start-up dental business, the key metrics I recommend that you measure are:

- Average Production Per Patient – seeing lots of patients does not necessarily translate into profitability.

  You are most efficient when you are providing the maximum amount of dentistry per patient appointment. I have found that your benchmark goal here should be on average $800 in production per active patient per year. An active patient is one that has attended your practice in the last 18 months.

- Total Production – this is a measure of income revenue and is used to derive other benchmark metrics. I typically only include collections in this metric, as I prefer using a cash accounting method.
  If you have significant income from

third party payers like dental insurance companies you will likely need to use an accrual accounting method. If this is the case you will want to include a separate "collections" metric to make sure you're actually getting paid. If you do measure collections your benchmark should be an average of 98% billings collected over a rolling three-month period.

- Consumables Costs – this includes costs for restorative materials, sterilization materials, etc. and is one of the few variable costs that you can realistically control. I generally recommend that consumables costs should be in the order of around 5% of practice income revenue.

If your consumables costs are consistently above 5% of revenue you might want to negotiate with your current supplier, change suppliers or consider becoming part of a buying group to negotiate group volume pricing.

- Dental Laboratory Costs - generally high margin dentistry like crown and bridge involves some form of laboratory work. Like consumables costs, you can control laboratory costs to a high degree. I recommend a benchmark of no more than 10% of revenue being spent on dental laboratory fees.

If your laboratory fees are consistently above this benchmark you may wish to negotiate with your preferred laboratory, consider a new outsourced laboratory, or if you do a lot of laboratory work, you could bring the work in-house and employ a dental ceramist or technician.

- Labor costs - this metric measures

the costs of employing support staff. Support staff are staff members who are not paid according to their production, and includes dental nurses, receptionists and administration staff. The benchmark I recommend for labor costs for support staff is between 25-30% of income revenue.

I personally tend to lean towards the higher end of this range, as I prefer to pay more to get the best people. Doing this is usually a long term cost savings through reduced staff turnover and improved morale.

- Number of new patients - this metric gives a great indication of how well your marketing and referral pathways are performing. Bearing in mind that the average patient attrition rate is around 15% in the dental industry, your benchmark for new patients should be around 15-20% per year.

If you are falling short of this figure, a closer examination of your marketing and referral channels is warranted. Perhaps advertising through conventional channels is necessary or developing a social media presence to drive your content marketing strategy is appropriate for your market. Implementing a referral scheme for existing patients may work for you.

- Total overheads – this is a measure of your total costs before remuneration to dentists. I suggest that you should aim to keep your overheads under 59%.

Comparing your dental business to the industry norm is fine in the early stages of your business or if you are simply trying to play "catch-up" with your peers, but be aware that it won't turn your business into a market leader. To become an industry leader, you must engage in "next practice" thinking: imagining what the future will look like and developing processes and capabilities to capitalize on these opportunities.

The benchmarking of processes and metrics not only gives you an understanding of how the processes and other metrics compare to industry leaders, but by extension provides you an insight into the areas of your business in need of improvement. By improving processes and by extension the metrics they give rise to, you can achieve improvements in efficiency, cost reductions and ultimately increased business equity.

CHAPTER FOURTEEN:
Corporate Branding

An important and perhaps one of the most enjoyable and exciting aspects of starting your new business is creating a brand. However, branding is much more than choosing a catchy name or creating a beautiful logo. Rather, your branding is the distillation of your business's strategy, values, vision, mission and goals. It pulls everything together and articulates your business's message to your market audience.

CHAPTER FOURTEEN: Corporate Branding

The ultimate purpose of branding is to create a loyal "tribe" of patients. A strong brand helps to shield you against patient attrition and can become a valuable asset in its own right – think of Coca Cola and Apple. So how do you go about building and developing your brand?

I am a big believer in developing your brand according to brand "archetypes". Using a brand archetype helps you to quickly establish a strong sense of identity, especially one that reflects the hopes and aspirations of your target audience. You will have identified your target audience earlier when you performed your market and demographic analysis. There are twelve brand archetypes around which to build your business's "personality":

- The innocent – this archetype represents the desire to be happy and free. Patients that relate to this archetype prefer straight-talking advertising and respond well to branding that promises simplicity.

- The hero - this archetype represents the desire to be brave and skillful. Patients that relate to the hero archetype value quality and efficiency. Your brand message should promote a high level of quality and your superiority versus your competitors.

- The everyman - the key driver of this archetype is to belong, and this is reflected in the values of patients who relate to it. They value friendliness and dependability. Your brand message should focus on belonging and honesty.

- The nurturer - this archetype is driven by protecting and caring for others. Patients that relate to this archetype respond to messages around safety and protection. Your brand message should consistently promise recognition.

- The dreamer - this archetype seeks to create something that is exceptional and lasting. This archetype generally does not respond well to advertising messages, but if your target audience are dreamers your message should promise authenticity.

- The explorer - this archetype seeks discovery and loathes conformity. Explorer patients respond well to messages that invite them to come on a journey with you, and you should convey a message of freedom.

- The rebel - this archetype is driven by revolution and is characterized as being unconventional. Your message to these patients should position your brand as being the alternative to the mainstream competitors and focus on promising a revolution.

- The lover - this archetype is driven by passion and pleasure. These patients value the esthetic appearance of services and products. Your message to this audience should promise a premium experience and focus on emotion and passion.

- The magician - this archetype is driven and seeks to understand the world around them. They value services they believe will make them wiser through their use. Your brand message should promise knowledge.

- The ruler - this archetype is driven to control and is afraid of chaos. Patients that respond to this archetype respond well to advertising that conveys the message that by using a particular service or product that they are superior to others. Your brand message should focus on promising power.

- The comedian - sometimes called the fool, this archetype is driven to live in the moment. These patients respond to branding which is playful and whimsical. Your message should promise an entertainment factor.

- The sage - like all wise men, this archetype is driven by the need to find wisdom. These patients will respond best to messages that uses more abstract symbolism and complex vocabulary. Your message to this audience should promise wisdom and knowledge.

This list of archetypes do tend to have an element of overlap, just as you will likely be seeking to get your message out to a broad audience. My advice to you is that your target audience should not be "everyone". The reality is that not everyone who could be possible buyers of dental services will use your dental business - quite simply it is virtually impossible to capture the entire market.

Instead, focus on getting your brand message out to no more than three archetypes - provided that they are not dramatically incompatible. For example, trying to send a consistent brand message to the rebel and nurturer archetypes who are essentially driven by polar opposite needs will simply create confusion. Remember that a confused patient becomes someone else's patient.

Your business brand message is typically conveyed in three ways:

- Visually - in the colors, symbols and images you choose for your brand. For example, the color orange conveys friendliness and incorporating the color in a logo is a good choice for a dental business that wants to primarily send a brand message to the everyman archetype. The discount shoe store Payless Shoesource makes extensive use of orange in its brand.

- Verbally - in the words and vocabulary you use in your messaging. You should aim to capture what drives your audience with your verbal message. For example if brand is the lover archetype, words that are emotive should feature strongly in your message. Whereas if your brand is the sage archetype, there will likely be a strong preference for highly objective, factual language.

- Experientially - by drawing together the promises you have made to your patients through your vision, mission, values, strategy and the words you use in your messages and advertisements. This is your opportunity to create a "proof point" for your patient and involves not only your service offerings but also how your business and staff interact with the patient and each other in the patient's eyes.

As you develop your business brand keep in mind that it should reflect your business's vision, mission and values, and it should be relatable to the aspirations and dreams of your target audience. Remember, branding is about sending the right message to the right audience at the right time.

CONCLUSION:
Next Steps

In the preceding pages we've covered the fundamental knowledge necessary for you to begin the journey to starting your own dental business. In each chapter I have made several recommendations and suggested activities that I believe are useful for beginning not only a dental business but have application in starting any business.

CONCLUSION: Next Steps

So what are the next steps? Well, if you have been actively engaged in the suggested activities, you will already have the blueprint for a business case. You will have an idea of your overall business strategy, you will have conducted a basic demographic, psychographic and competitor analysis and have the necessary information around professional fees necessary to generate financial projections.

Utilizing SMART goal setting techniques you will be able to develop objectives and milestones to guide your progress to beginning your business, including having some guidelines on what to look for when scoping out potential locations for your business. You will now have a basic understanding of the key financial statements and can be an active participant with your chosen accountant when discussing finances related to your business.

The hiring model I have presented will help you to recruit and efficiently organize the best team members for your business. You also now have the knowledge of key industry metrics against which you can benchmark your business and plan improvements. You will also have the basic knowledge to develop a corporate brand and the specific message elements you should convey to your target audience. These elements all form part of a business plan.

Developing and refining your business plan should then be the next step you take. Woody Allen, said: "80 percent of success is just showing up." I like to refine this by adding: "If 80 percent of success is showing up, then 90 percent of success is showing up with a plan, and 99% of success is showing up with a plan and consistently implementing it. The rest is plain luck."

A final thought on starting a business, and one that is especially important for those coming from a technical background: "You will make mistakes and you will fail." The key is learning from your mistakes and developing the resilience to push through. Paul Graham, the co-founder of Y Combinator, perfectly, albeit crudely, sums up the professional and emotional trials of starting a business and offers some great advice: "Bad shit is coming. It always is in a startup. The odds of getting from launch to liquidity without some kind of disaster happening are one in a thousand. So don't get demoralized."

I would like to thank you for allowing me to be a part of your journey from technical worker to business owner. I wish you and your new business all the success in world. And finally: "Good luck and let's start something!"

www.ingramcontent.com/pod-product-compliance
Lightning Source LLC
Chambersburg PA
CBHW052014230326
41598CB00078B/3419